101 Things To Do With Powdered Milk

101 Things To Do With Powdered Milk

BY
DARLENE CARLISLE

GIBBS SMITH
TO ENRICH AND INSPIRE HUMANKIND

First Edition
17 16 15 14 13   5 4 3 2 1

Text © 2013 Darlene Carlisle

101 Things is a registered trademark of Gibbs Smith,
Publisher and Stephanie Ashcraft.

All rights reserved. No part of this book may be reproduced by
any means whatsoever without written permission from the
publisher, except brief portions quoted for purpose of review.

Published by
Gibbs Smith
P.O. Box 667
Layton, Utah 84041

1.800.835.4993 orders
www.gibbs-smith.com

Gibbs Smith books are printed on either recycled, 100% post-consumer waste, FSC-certified papers or on paper produced from sustainable PEFC-certified forest/controlled wood source. Learn more at www.pefc.org.

Library of Congress Cataloging-in-Publication Data

Carlisle, Darlene.
  101 things to do with powdered milk / Darlene Carlisle. — First edition.
     pages cm
  ISBN 978-1-4236-3287-0
1. Cooking. 2. Dried milk. I. Title. II. Title: One hundred
one things to do with powdered milk. III. Title: One
hundred and one things to do with powdered milk.
  TX714.C3731547 2013
  641.6'7143—dc23

                                                              2012032634

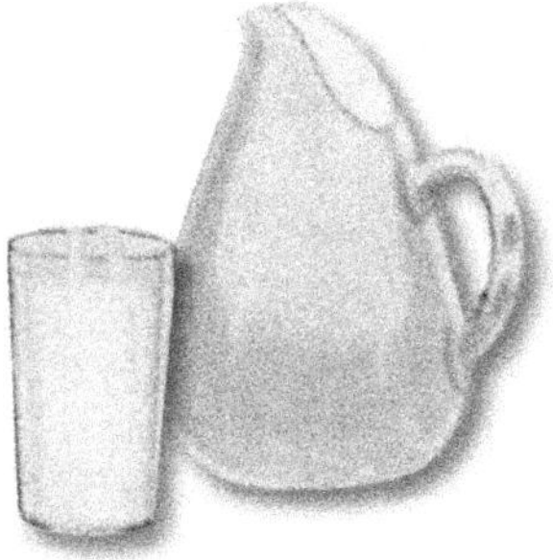

Yum!

More recipes and tips
at 101yum.com

CONTENTS

Helpful Hints 9

Yogurt, Milks, Creams & Cheeses

Powdered Milk Yogurt 12 • Powdered Milk Yogurt Sour Cream 13 • Powdered Milk Yogurt Cream Cheese 14 • Powdered Milk Buttermilk 15 • Quick Powdered Milk Buttermilk or Sour Milk 16 • Powdered Milk Evaporated Milk 17 • Powdered Milk Sweetened Condensed Milk 18 • Easy Powdered Milk Whipped Topping 19 • Powdered Milk Whipped Topping 20 • Powdered Milk Cottage Cheese 21 • Powdered Milk Baker's Cheese 22 • Powdered Milk Sour Cream 23 • Powdered Milk Day Cheese 24 • Powdered Milk Mozzarella Cheese 25

Favorite Drinks

Banana Milk 28 • Spice Milk 29 • Grape Milk 30 • Cocoa Chocolate Milk Mix 31 • Banana Nut Smoothie 32 • Health Smoothie 33 • Strawberry Banana Yogurt Smoothie 34 • Brazilian Lemonade 35

Breads

1 Hour Bread 38 • Cornbread 39 • Almond Bread 40 • Dinner Rolls 41 • Scones 42 • Baking Powder Biscuits 43 • Homemade Biscuit Mix 44 • Waffles 46 • Nut and Grain Pancakes 47 • Oatmeal Pancakes 48 • German Puffy Pancakes 49 • French Breakfast Puffs 50

Dips & Spreads

Curried Yogurt Dip 52 • Cucumber Dill Dip or Sauce 53 • Spinach Artichoke Dip 54 • Layered Mexican Dip 55 • Salmon Cheese Spread 56 • Shrimp Spread 57 • Fresh Cheese with Chives 58 • Cinnamon Spread 59 • Cheese Ball 60 • Buttermilk Maple Syrup 61

Sauces, Soups & Salads

Allemande Sauce 64 • Alfredo Sauce 65 • Thin, Medium, and Thick White Sauce 66 • Creamed Eggs 68 • Black Bean Soup 69 • Rich Potato Soup 70 • Scalloped Potato Soup 71 • Broccoli-Cheddar Soup 72 • Corn Chowder 73 • Shrimp and Clam Chowder 74 • Apple Salad 75 • Cranberry Waldorf Salad 76

Main Dishes

Stroganoff 78 • Easy Taco Pie 79 • Beefy Enchiladas 80 • Chicken Enchiladas 81 • Baked Chicken Taquitos 82 • Quick Chicken Alfredo 83 • Three-Cheese Chicken Lasagna 84 • Chicken Pot Pie 85 • Chicken Lik-Dop 86 • Lasagna 87 • Faux Fettuccine 88 • Cheesy Meatball Skillet 89 • Tuna Crunch Pie 90 • Garden-Stuffed Baked Potatoes 91 • Hash-brown Sausage Bake 92 • Breakfast Omelet Casserole 93 • Quiche a la Lorraine 94

Desserts & Treats

Crepes 96 • Baked Cheesecake 97 • Easy Cheesecake 98 • Yogurt Streusel Coffee Cake 99 • Lemon Yogurt Cake 100 • Cream Cheese Frosting 101 • Basic Cookie Mix 102 • Oatmeal Cookies 103 • Peanut Butter Cookies 104 • Lemon Drop Cookies 105 • Cinnamon Cookies 106 • Pecan Tassies 107 • Rocky Road Cornflake Cookies 108 • Fruit Supreme Pie 109 • Pudding and Pie Filling 110 • Bread Pudding 112 • Rice Pudding 113 • Apple Kuchen 114 • Frozen Yogurt 115 • Lemon Frozen Yogurt 116 • Caramel 117 • Licorice Caramels 118 • Fudge Kisses 119 • Peanut Butter Fudge 120 • Peanut Butter Sesame Balls 121 • Peanut Butter Chews 122 • Tootsie Rolls 123 • Honey Mints 124

HELPFUL HINTS

1. You would be surprised at how many commercial food items you eat every day that have powdered milk in them, from yogurts and cottage cheese to nutrition bars. This cookbook will show you how to make many of the same foods, and at a fraction of the cost.

2. Powdered milk is such an easy thing to store and use. It can be used in your everyday cooking and is a wonderful food to take camping, eliminating the need to keep a jug of fresh milk.

3. There are three types of powdered milk; non-fat dry, non-fat dry instant, and whey.

4. Powdered milk stores well when packaged properly and kept at room temperature or cooler. Milk stored in airtight, low-oxygen cans has been found to last longer and stay fresher tasting than milk stored in boxes or plastic bags. It can be stored for up to twenty years, but should be used before then.

5. If you are substituting powdered milk for fresh milk in a recipe, add the powdered milk to the dry ingredients then just add water where it calls for milk.

6. The easiest way to mix powdered milk is in your blender. With the blender setting on low, pour in the water and turn on then add the powdered milk and turn off as soon as it is mixed in. If you blend for too long, you'll create too much foam.

7. Some people find it easy to mix up a gallon at a time and keep it in the refrigerator for use like you would milk in any recipe.

8. When using yogurt in recipes, fold, do not stir into other ingredients and it will keep the original consistency. Do not beat or whip.

9. Spare the heat in cooking with yogurt. Low temperatures and short heating times are the best. Yogurt may separate.

10. Plain yogurt can be substituted for sour cream in recipes like Beef Stroganoff or Swedish Meatballs by adding 1 tablespoon of cornstarch or 2 tablespoons flour per cup of yogurt.

11. Replace the sour cream called for in cakes and cookies with plain or vanilla yogurt. Add 1 teaspoon baking soda to dry ingredients with other leavening in recipe.

12. Use yogurt instead of milk or cream in mashed potatoes and pasta dishes, and replace buttermilk in biscuits and pancakes with yogurt thinned with a little water.

All recipes in this book are formulated using the LDS Home Storage non-fat dry milk.

To make 1 quart milk, combine 4 cups water with the below:

LDS Home storage	Non-fat dry	3/4 cup
Rainy Day Foods	Non-fat dry	1/2 cup
Country Cream	Instant	2/3 cup
Great Value	Instant	1 1/3 cups
Country Fresh	Instant	1 1/3 cups
Morning Moo	Whey/non-fat dry	1/2 cup

To make 1 gallon milk, combine 15 cups water with the below:

LDS Home storage	Non-fat dry	3 cups
Rainy Day Foods	Non-fat dry	2 cups
Country Cream	Instant	2 2/3 cups
Great Value	Instant	5 1/3 cups
Country Fresh	Instant	5 1/3 cups
Morning Moo	Whey/non-fat dry	2 cups

YOGURT, MILKS, CREAMS & CHEESES

POWDERED MILK YOGURT

7 cups	**warm water,** divided
2 1/2 cups	**powdered milk**
1 package	**Knox unflavored gelatin,** optional*
1/2 cup or 1 container (6 ounces)	**plain yogurt****

Pour 3 cups water into a blender, turn on low, and add the remaining ingredients. Blend just until mixed. Add the remaining water and stir. Pour into a yogurt maker. Process for 4–6 hours or until set (do not go over 12 hours). When it is set (coagulated), refrigerate. It will continue to thicken. Makes 2 quarts.

*The gelatin helps it set up faster and firmer.

**You can use yogurt enzymes purchased from your local health food store.

NOTE: I recommend using a yogurt maker, but if you want to do it without one, pour into pint jars, put lids on, and place jars into a pan or cooler. Fill with hot water to the neck of the jar. Water should be and stay at the temperature range of 105–115 degrees. Place on a hot pad, wrap in towels, or set in the sun.

POWDERED MILK YOGURT SOUR CREAM

7 cups	**warm water,** divided
3¾ cups	**powdered milk**
1 package	**Knox unflavored gelatin,** optional*
½ cup or 1 container (6 ounces)	**plain yogurt****

Pour 3 cups water into a blender, turn on low, and add the remaining ingredients. Blend just until mixed. Add the remaining water and stir. Pour into a yogurt maker. Process for 4–6 hours or until set (do not go over 12 hours). When it is set (coagulated), refrigerate. It will continue to thicken. Makes 2 quarts.

*The gelatin helps it set up faster and firmer.

**You can use yogurt enzymes purchased from your local health food store.

NOTE: I recommend using a yogurt maker, but if you want to do it without one, pour into pint jars, put lids on, and place jars into a pan or cooler. Fill with hot water to the neck of the jar. Water should be and stay at the temperature range of 105–115 degrees. Place on a hot pad, wrap in towels, or set in the sun.

POWDERED MILK YOGURT CREAM CHEESE

5 1/4 cups	**lukewarm water,** divided
3 3/4 cups	**powdered milk**
1/2 to 1 cup	**plain yogurt***

Pour 3 cups water into a blender, turn on low, and add the remaining ingredients. Blend just until mixed. Add the remaining water and stir. Pour into a yogurt maker. Process for 4–6 hours or until set.

When coagulated, place into a strainer lined with cheese cloth and drain overnight, or until the desired consistency.

You can knead it if you want a smooth texture. Measure into 1 cup portions then place into storage containers. Refrigerate. It also freezes well. Makes 5–6 cups.

* You can use yogurt enzymes purchased from your local health food store.

POWDERED MILK BUTTERMILK

3 cups	**warm water**
1 cup	**powdered milk**
1/2 cup	**buttermilk or 3 tablespoons buttermilk powder**

Pour the water into a blender, turn on low, and add dry ingredients. Mix in buttermilk (if not using powdered) and pour into a large jar. Cover and put in a warm place until clabbered (thickened). It will take anywhere from 5–10 hours. Then refrigerate.

Save the last 1/2 cup to start another batch. Occasionally add fresh buttermilk or powder to keep it fresh. Buttermilk will last for 2–3 weeks in the refrigerator. Makes 1 quart.

QUICK POWDERED MILK BUTTERMILK OR SOUR MILK

1 cup	**water lukewarm**
1/3 cup	**powdered milk**
1 tablespoon	**vinegar or lemon juice**

Mix the water and powdered milk in a blender on low, just until mixed. Add the vinegar or lemon juice to the milk and stir. Let set for 5 minutes so it can curdle. Makes 1 1/4 cups.

POWDERED MILK EVAPORATED MILK

1 cup **water**
²/₃ cup **powdered milk**

Mix the water and powdered milk in a blender on low, or slowly add the water to the powdered milk; stir until smooth. Makes 1 ¼ cups.

POWDERED MILK SWEETENED CONDENSED MILK

1/2 cup	**hot water**
4 tablespoons	**butter**
3/4 cup	**powdered milk**
3/4 cup	**sugar**

Mix the water and butter in a blender on low and add the powdered milk and sugar, blending until smooth. Makes 1 1/2 cups.

EASY POWDERED MILK WHIPPED TOPPING

2/3 cup	**powdered milk**
3/4 cup	**ice water,** divided
1/2 cup	**powdered sugar**
1 teaspoon	**vanilla**

Chill a medium bowl and beaters. Add the powdered milk to the bowl and a little of the water to make a creamy paste then add the rest of the water and sugar. Whip until fluffy. This will take 5–10 minutes. Add the vanilla and whip until blended and fluffy. This will keep in the refrigerator. Whip to re-fluff, if needed. Makes 2 1/2 cups.

POWDERED MILK WHIPPED TOPPING

1 cup	**water**
1/4 cup plus 2 tablespoons	**powdered milk**
2 teaspoons	**Knox unflavored gelatin**
1 1/2 tablespoons	**cold water**
1/4 cup	**sugar**
1 teaspoon	**vanilla**

Pour 1 cup water into a blender, turn on low, and add powdered milk, blending until just mixed. Then place milk in a small saucepan, or in a bowl in the microwave, and heat until scalding.

In a small bowl, soak the gelatin in cold water. Combine the gelatin, scalded milk, and sugar in a medium bowl; stirring well. Place in refrigerator and chill until it jells, but is not firmly set.

Beat this mixture until it is the consistency of whipped cream. This will take 5–10 minutes. Add the vanilla and whip until stiff peaks form. This needs to be used right away because it has gelatin in it and will set up quickly. Makes approximately 3 cups.

NOTE: Recipe courtesy of Utah State University Extension.

POWDERED MILK COTTAGE CHEESE

1/2	**rennet tablet***
1 teaspoon	**citric acid,** optional
8 cups	**warm water,** divided
3 cups	**powdered milk**
1/2 cup	**Powdered Milk Buttermilk** (page 15)
1/2 to 1 teaspoon	**salt**

In a large bowl, dissolve the rennet and citric acid, if using, in 5 cups water.

Pour the remaining water in a blender, turn on low, and add the powdered milk and buttermilk. Blend only until mixed, do not over mix or you will create foam. Add to rennet water and stir. Let set at room temperature, around 70 degrees, for 12–16 hours.

When firm, cut into cubes in the bowl and set the bowl in a sink of hot water (110 degrees). Gently stir every few minutes to evenly warm. After about 10–20 minutes, the curds and whey will start to separate. Pour the mixture into a cheesecloth-lined strainer and drain then rinse with cold water to set the curd and rinse out the whey. Season with salt and gently mix in. If you want it to have the creamy consistency of store-bought cottage cheese, add milk or cream to it. Chill completely before eating. Makes 1 1/2 quarts.

*Rennet is an enzyme that usually comes from a calf stomach. Most of the rennet sold in stores is plant based and vegetarian. It often can be found near the gelatin at your local grocery store, or you can order it online or find it at a health foods store.

POWDERED MILK BAKER'S CHEESE

1/2	**rennet tablet***
1 teaspoon	**citric acid,** optional
8 cups	**warm water,** divided
3 cups	**powdered milk**
1/2 cup	**Powdered Milk Buttermilk** (page 15)
1/2 to 1 teaspoon	**salt**

In a large bowl, dissolve the rennet and citric acid, if using, in 5 cups water.

Pour the remaining water in a blender, turn on low, and add the powdered milk and buttermilk. Blend only until mixed, do not over mix or you will create foam. Add to rennet water and stir. Let set at room temperature, around 70 degrees, for 12–16 hours. When firm, drain in a cheesecloth-lined strainer and squeeze or drain until the consistency of cream cheese. Season with salt and gently mix in. Refrigerate or freeze. Makes approximately 1 quart.

*Rennet is an enzyme that usually comes from a calf stomach. Most of the rennet sold in stores is plant based and vegetarian. It often can be found near the gelatin at your local grocery store, or you can order it online or find it at a health foods store.

POWDERED MILK SOUR CREAM

1/2	**rennet tablet***
1 teaspoon	**citric acid,** optional
8 cups	**warm water,** divided
3 cups	**powdered milk**
1/2 cup	**Powdered Milk Buttermilk** (page 15)
1/2 to 1 teaspoon	**salt**

In a large bowl, dissolve the rennet and citric acid, if using, in 5 cups water.

Pour the remaining water in a blender, turn on low, and add the powdered milk and buttermilk. Blend only until mixed, do not over mix or you will create foam. Add to rennet water and stir. Let set at room temperature, around 70 degrees, for 12-16 hours.

When firm, cut into cubes in the bowl and set the bowl in a sink of hot water (110 degrees). Gently stir every few minutes to evenly warm. After about 10-20 minutes, the curds and whey will start to separate. Pour the mixture into a cheesecloth-lined strainer and drain then rinse with cold water to set the curd and rinse out the whey. Season with salt and gently mix in. Spoon into a blender and blend until smooth and creamy. Chill. Makes approximately 1 1/2 quarts.

*Rennet is an enzyme that usually comes from a calf stomach. Most of the rennet sold in stores is plant based and vegetarian. It often can be found near the gelatin at your local grocery store, or you can order it online or find it at a health foods store.

POWDERED MILK DAY CHEESE

4 cups	**water**
1 1/2 cups	**powdered milk**
3 tablespoons	**lemon juice or vinegar**
	salt, to taste

Mix water and powdered milk in a blender, just until blended. Then pour into a medium saucepan and slowly warm the milk over a low heat. Pour the lemon juice or vinegar into it at a drizzle. Bring just to the point of boiling. If it hasn't separated into curds and whey, add some more lemon juice or vinegar. Never bring it to a boil. When it has separated, drain in a cheesecloth-lined strainer and rinse with cold water. Add salt, to taste. Makes 2 cups.

NOTE: This can be used as a substitute in recipes calling for ricotta cheese.

POWDERED MILK MOZZARELLA CHEESE

3 cups	**powdered milk**
14 cups	**water**
1 to 2 cups	**cream or half-and-half or $^1/_2$ cup oil**
$^1/_2$	**rennet tablet***
$^1/_4$ cup	**cold water**
2 teaspoons	**citric acid**
1 to 2 teaspoon	**pure salt** (no iodine or anti-caking agents)

Combine powdered milk and 14 cups water in a large pitcher; refrigerate overnight.

Add cream or half-and-half to milk. If using oil, blend with some of the milk to get it mixed in well and then add back into the rest of the milk. Crush the rennet tablet and place it in a small bowl. Add 1/4 cup water to dissolve; set aside.

Pour the milk into a large stainless steel pot and warm over medium heat. Sprinkle citric acid into the milk and stir gently. Heat slowly to 88 degrees, you will start to see the milk curdle. Between 88–90 degrees, add the rennet water, stir for 30 seconds until well mixed, then let set until the temperature reaches 105 degrees. Turn off the heat. You should now have a solid mass with whey around the edges. Either cut it into cubes or stir gently to break it up.

continued

Ladle curds into a large microwave-safe bowl. Microwave on high for 1 minute, drain off whey, and then knead cheese into a ball until it cools a little. You will need to use heavy rubber gloves when kneading the hot cheese to prevent burning your hands. Add salt. Microwave for 30–35 seconds, drain off whey, and knead again, stretching the cheese like taffy.

The cheese is done when it is smooth and shiny and pliable. You might need to microwave one more time for 30 seconds. Eat now or shape into a ball, wrap in plastic wrap, and refrigerate. Makes approximately 3 cups.

*Rennet is an enzyme that usually comes from a calf stomach. Most of the rennet sold in stores is plant based and vegetarian. It often can be found near the gelatin at your local grocery store, or you can order it online or find it at a health foods store.

FAVORITE DRINKS

BANANA MILK

1 cup	**water**
1/4 cup	**powdered milk**
2	**ripe bananas**
1 cup	**milk**

Pour water into a blender, turn on low, and add the powdered milk, bananas, and milk; blending until smooth. Chill. Makes 3 cups.

NOTE: Recipe courtesy of Utah State University Extension.

SPICE MILK

2 cups	**powdered milk**
1 tablespoon	**sugar**
1/2 teaspoon	**cinnamon**
1/4 teaspoon	**salt**
1/2 teaspoon	**nutmeg**
1 1/2 quarts	**milk,** divided

Combine dry ingredients in a small bowl. Pour half of the milk into a 2-quart pitcher and the rest into a blender. Turn blender on low and add the dry ingredients. Blend for 15–30 seconds, until mixed, then add to the pitcher; stir to mix. Chill. Makes 1 1/2 quarts.

NOTE: Recipe courtesy of Utah State University Extension.

GRAPE MILK

2 cups	**water**
1 cup	**powdered milk**
1 cup	**milk**
2 1/4 cups	**grape juice**

Pour water into a blender, turn on low, and add powdered milk, milk, and juice. Blend for 15–30 seconds and chill before serving. Makes 6 cups.

NOTE: Recipe courtesy of Utah State University Extension.

COCOA CHOCOLATE MILK MIX

1 cup	**baking cocoa powder**
1/2 teaspoon	**salt**
4 cups	**instant powdered milk**
3/4 cup	**sugar**

Combine ingredients and store in tightly covered container.

To use: Add 1/4 cup mix to 1 cup hot water. Makes 20 cups of cocoa.

NOTE: Recipe courtesy of Utah State University Extension.

BANANA NUT SMOOTHIE

1	**banana,** fresh or frozen
1 cup	**Powdered Milk Yogurt** (page 12)
1/4 cup	**walnuts**
1/2 teaspoon	**cinnamon**
1 teaspoon	**honey**
1/4 teaspoon	**vanilla or almond extract**
	nutmeg, to taste

Cut banana into 3 or 4 chunks; place in a blender with the remaining ingredients except the nutmeg. Blend until smooth. Serve with a sprinkle with nutmeg. Makes 2 cups.

HEALTH SMOOTHIE

1 cup	**apple juice or coconut water**
1 cup	**Powdered Milk Yogurt** (page 12)
1/4 cup	**flax meal**
1 cup	**fresh spinach**
1	**banana**
1 teaspoon	**lemon-flavor cod liver oil***
1 tablespoon	**molasses**
1 cup	**fresh or frozen strawberries and blueberries**
1 teaspoon to 1 tablespoon	**green powder***

Mix all ingredients in blender on high until smooth. Makes 3 1/2 cups.

*Found in health foods stores.

STRAWBERRY BANANA YOGURT SMOOTHIE

1 1/2 cups	**frozen strawberries**
1	**banana**
1 cup	**Powdered Milk Yogurt** (page 12)
1/2 cup	**unsweetened apple juice or orange juice**
1/2 cup	**water**

Place all ingredients in a blender and blend until smooth. Makes 3 cups.

VARIATION: Can also be put into cups or molds and frozen to make popsicles.

BRAZILIAN LEMONADE

1 cup	**sugar**
6 cups	**water**
2	**lemons**
2	**limes**
1/3 cup	**Powdered Milk Sweetened Condensed Milk** (page 18)
	crushed ice

Mix the sugar and water together in a medium pitcher until dissolved.

Wash the lemons and limes really well and then cut each into quarters. In a blender, blend half of the fruit with a fourth of the sugar water for about 15–30 seconds.

Pour the mixture through a strainer into a large pitcher. Repeat with the remaining fruit. Pour the remaining sugar water over the fruit pulp in the strainer and drain for a few minutes. Remove strainer and mix in the condensed milk. Serve over crushed ice. Makes 7 cups.

BREADS

1 HOUR BREAD

9 cups	**bread flour**
1 1/2 cups	**rolled oats**
1/2 cup	**ground, crushed, or chopped flax seeds**
3/4 cup	**powdered milk**
1/4 cup	**instant yeast**
1 tablespoon	**salt**
4 cups	**warm water**
3 tablespoons	**liquid lecithin**
1	**egg,** optional

Preheat oven to 350 degrees.

Mix dry ingredients together in bowl of mixer until blended. Add water, lecithin, and egg, if using, and mix for about 6 minutes. The dough should be slightly sticky. Add more flour or water, as needed. Place on greased countertop and shape into loaves, rolls, or breadsticks. Place dough in pans that have been prepared with nonstick cooking spray and let rise for 30 minutes.

Bake bread loaves for 25–30 minutes, rolls for 18–20 minutes, and breadsticks until golden brown. Makes approximately 4 loaves, 32–48 rolls, or 18–24 breadsticks.

VARIATION: I love to use this recipe for pizza crusts and calzones. When doing pizza crusts, I roll out the dough, brush it with some garlic-seasoned melted butter, then bake for 5 minutes at 450 degrees. Remove from oven, cover with sauce and toppings, then bake again for 10 minutes or more depending on the thickness of the dough.

CORNBREAD

1 cup	**butter,** softened
1 cup	**sugar**
2	**eggs**
1 1/2 cups	**flour**
1 cup	**cornmeal**
4 1/2 tablespoons	**powdered milk**
2 teaspoons	**baking powder**
2 teaspoons	**salt**
1 1/2 cups	**water**

Preheat oven to 350 degrees.

In a large bowl, cream the butter and sugar together until well combined. Add the eggs and continue creaming. Add remaining ingredients and mix well.

Pour batter into a 9 x 9-inch pan that has been prepared with nonstick cooking spray and bake for 40 minutes, or until a toothpick inserted in the center comes out clean. Makes 8 servings.

ALMOND BREAD

3 1/4 cups	**flour**
2 teaspoons	**baking powder**
1 teaspoon	**baking soda**
2 cups	**brown sugar**
6 tablespoons	**grated orange peel**
1/2 pound	**sliced or chopped almonds**
2 cups	**whipped Powdered Milk Yogurt** (page 12)

Preheat oven to 350 degrees.

In a large bowl, combine the flour, baking powder, and baking soda. Add remaining ingredients and mix well for about 2–3 minutes. Pour batter into a loaf pan or 10-inch round cake pan that has been prepared with nonstick cooking spray and floured. Bake for 50–60 minutes, or until a toothpick inserted in the center comes out clean. Makes 12 servings.

DINNER ROLLS

3 1/2 cups	**flour,** divided
2 teaspoons	**active dry yeast**
1 1/4 cups	**water**
1/4 cup	**powdered milk**
1/4 cup	**sugar**
1/4 cup	**olive oil**
1 teaspoon	**salt**
1	**egg**

Preheat oven to 400 degrees.

Add 1 1/2 cups flour and yeast to mixer bowl and blend together.

Mix water and powdered milk together in a blender on low until well combined. Then place milk in a small saucepan and add sugar, oil, and salt. Heat and stir until warm (115–120 degrees) and remove from heat. (You can heat in the microwave for 1–1 1/2 minutes.) Add milk to dry ingredients and mix to combine. Add egg and mix until blended and then beat at high speed for 3 minutes. Stir in remaining flour to make a soft dough.

Shape dough into a ball and place in a greased large bowl; turn dough in the bowl to grease the surface. Cover and let rise in a warm place until double in size, about 1 1/2–2 hours.

When dough has doubled, punch down, turn out onto a lightly floured surface, shape into a ball, cover, and let rest for 10 minutes. Shape into desired rolls, place on a baking sheet or muffin tin that has been prepared with nonstick cooking spray, cover, and let rise in warm place for 30–45 minutes. Bake for 10–12 minutes. Makes 12 large rolls or 24 small dinner rolls.

NOTE: You can use this dough to make bread sticks and cinnamon rolls.

SCONES

2 teaspoons	**active dry yeast**
2 cups	**Powdered Milk Buttermilk** (page 15), warmed
6 tablespoons	**cooking oil**
1	**egg**
4 cups	**flour**
1 tablespoon	**sugar**
1 1/2 teaspoons	**baking powder**
1/2 teaspoon	**salt**
1/2 teaspoon	**baking soda**

In a large bowl, dissolve yeast in the buttermilk then whisk in oil and egg. Add dry ingredients, mix, and then knead dough for a few minutes until smooth. Place dough in a greased large bowl, cover, and refrigerate overnight.

In a large frying pan, preheat about 1-inch cooking oil to 350 degrees. Roll dough out on a lightly floured surface. Cut and stretch individual pieces sized for small scones or Navajo tacos. Fry scones in batches, cooking on both sides until golden brown. Serve with honey butter or stack with taco ingredients for Navajo tacos. Makes 24 small scones or 12 Navajo tacos.

BAKING POWDER BISCUITS

3 cups	**flour**
4 1/2 teaspoons	**baking powder**
3/4 teaspoon	**salt**
3/4 teaspoon	**cream of tartar**
2 1/2 tablespoons	**sugar**
3 tablespoons	**powdered milk**
3/4 cup	**shortening**
1	**egg**
1 cup	**water**

Preheat oven to 450 degrees.

In a large bowl, sift together dry ingredients. Cut in shortening. In a small bowl, beat egg lightly and add water then add to the dry mixture. Mix with a fork until the dough holds together. Knead gently about 20 times. Roll dough out on a lightly floured surface to a 1–2-inch-thick circle. Cut into biscuits.

Place on a baking sheet that has been prepared with nonstick cooking spray and bake for 8–10 minutes, or until lightly browned. Makes 12 biscuits.

HOMEMADE BISCUIT MIX

10 cups	**flour**
1/3 cup	**baking powder**
1/4 cup	**sugar**
4 teaspoons	**salt**
2 cups	**powdered milk**
2 cups	**shortening**

In a large bowl, combine dry ingredients. Cut in the shortening until the mixture resembles coarse crumbs. Store in an airtight container at room temperature. It will store for several weeks. Use in all sorts of recipes, just like you would use Bisquick. Makes 14 cups.

NOTE: Recipe courtesy of Tracey Lou Mullen.

BISCUITS

2 cups	**Homemade Biscuit Mix**
1/2 cup	**water**

Preheat oven to 450 degrees.

In a medium bowl, stir biscuit mix and water together with a fork just until dough is moistened and forms a ball. Turn dough out onto a lightly floured surface and knead 10 times. Roll out to 1/2–1 inch thickness and cut with biscuit or cookie cutter. Place on a baking sheet that has been prepared with nonstick cooking spray and bake for 10 minutes or until golden brown. Makes 8 biscuits.

PANCAKES

2	**eggs**
1 cup	**water**
2 cups	**Homemade Biscuit Mix**

Heat an electric griddle to 350 degrees. Prepare griddle with nonstick cooking spray.

Place all ingredients in a medium bowl and whisk together until smooth. Pour 1/4 cup batter per pancake evenly onto hot griddle. Cook for 1–2 minutes on each side until golden brown. Makes 12 (4-inch) pancakes.

MUFFINS

3 cups	**Homemade Biscuit Mix**
3 tablespoons	**sugar**
1	**egg,** beaten
1 cup	**water**

Preheat oven to 400 degrees.

In a large bowl, combine the biscuit mix and sugar. Add the egg and water and stir just until moistened and slightly lumpy. Line a muffin pan with paper liners or prepare with nonstick cooking spray and fill each cup 2/3 full. Bake for 20 minutes. Makes 12 muffins.

WAFFLES

2 cups	**flour**
2 tablespoons	**sugar**
1 tablespoon	**baking powder**
1 teaspoon	**salt**
6 tablespoons	**powdered milk**
1 3/4 cups	**water**
1/3 cup	**cooking oil**
2	**eggs**

Heat waffle iron and prepare with nonstick cooking spray.

In a large bowl, mix together the dry ingredients. In a small bowl, whisk together the water, oil, and eggs. Add to the dry ingredients and stir, just until blended.

Pour 1/3 cup batter onto waffle iron for each waffle. Bake for 5 minutes or until steaming stops and waffles are golden brown. Carefully remove waffles. Makes 12 (4-inch) waffles.

NUT AND GRAIN PANCAKES

³/₄ cup	**quick or regular oats**
³/₄ cup	**whole-wheat flour**
2 tablespoons	**flour**
2 teaspoons	**baking soda**
1 teaspoon	**baking powder**
¹/₂ teaspoon	**salt**
1 ¹/₂ cups	**Powdered Milk Buttermilk** (page 15)
¹/₄ cup	**cooking oil**
1	**egg**
¹/₄ cup	**sugar**
3 tablespoons	**finely chopped almonds**
3 tablespoons	**finely chopped walnuts**

Heat an electric griddle to 350 degrees. Prepare griddle with nonstick cooking spray. Place oats in a blender and blend on medium high until the consistency of flour.

In a small bowl, combine the dry ingredients, except sugar and nuts; set aside. In a medium bowl, mix together the buttermilk, oil, egg, and sugar with a hand mixer until smooth. Add dry ingredients and nuts and mix well. Pour ¹/₄ cup batter per pancake evenly onto hot griddle. Cook for 2–4 minutes on each side until golden brown. Makes 12 (4-inch) pancakes.

OATMEAL PANCAKES

1 1/2 cups	**oatmeal** (rolled oats or instant)
3/4 cup	**water**
2	**eggs**
2 tablespoons	**cooking oil**
2 tablespoons	**brown sugar**
1 tablespoon	**baking powder**
1/4 teaspoon	**salt**
1/4 cup powdered	**milk**

Heat an electric griddle to 350 degrees. Prepare griddle with nonstick cooking spray.

Place oatmeal in a blender and blend on medium high until the consistency of flour. Pour into a small bowl and set aside. Add water, eggs, and oil to the blender and turn on low, adding the rest of the ingredients including the oatmeal flour. Blend until smooth. Allow to stand for 5 minutes. If batter is too thick when ready to use, add just a little milk.

Pour 1/4 cup batter per pancake evenly onto hot griddle. Cook for 1-2 minutes on each side until golden brown. Makes 8 (4-inch) pancakes.

VARIATION: Add 1/4 cup of any mix of nuts, chopped or ground, to the batter when you add the oatmeal flour.

GERMAN PUFFY PANCAKES

6 tablespoons	**butter**
1 cup	**water**
6	**eggs**
3 tablespoons	**powdered milk**
1 cup	**flour**
1/4 teaspoon	**salt**
2 tablespoons	**sugar**
1 teaspoon	**vanilla**
	powdered sugar
	syrup or honey
	fruit

Preheat oven to 450 degrees.

Melt butter in a 9 x 13-inch pan in oven as it is preheating. Place water in a blender, turn on low, and add the rest of the ingredients until mixed. Add this mixture to the pan with melted butter and return to oven. Bake for 18 minutes. Do not open the oven during baking time. Pancake will be high and fluffy with browned edges when finished. Sprinkle with powdered sugar and serve with syrup, honey, or fruit. Makes 4–6 servings.

NOTE: If you omit the sugar and vanilla, it can be served with roast beef and gravy as a Yorkshire pudding.

FRENCH BREAKFAST PUFFS

1/3 cup	**butter,** softened
1/2 cup	**sugar**
1	**egg**
1 1/2 cups	**flour**
1 1/2 teaspoons	**baking powder**
1/2 teaspoon	**salt**
1/4 teaspoon	**nutmeg**
1 1/2 tablespoons	**powdered milk**
1/2 cup	**water**
1/2 cup	**sugar**
1 teaspoon	**cinnamon**
6 to 8 tablespoons	**butter,** melted

Preheat oven to 350 degrees.

In a large bowl, add the softened butter, sugar, and egg. Cream together until well incorporated. In a small bowl, sift together the dry ingredients and then add to the creamed butter alternately with the water. Mix until well combined.

In a small bowl, mix the sugar and cinnamon together and set aside.

Pour batter into a 12-cup muffin tin that has been prepared with nonstick cooking spray and bake for 20–25 minutes. Cool just enough so you can handle them, then roll the entire puff, or just the top, in melted butter then sugar mixture. Makes 12 puffs.

NOTE: You can add grated apples or carrots to the batter. You can also substitute 1/4 of the water with applesauce.

DIPS & SPREADS

CURRIED YOGURT DIP

1 1/4 cups	**mayonnaise**
1/3 cup	**Powdered Milk Yogurt** (page 12)
1/2 teaspoon	**curry powder**

Mix all ingredients together in a small bowl and refrigerate until ready to use. Serve with cut vegetables or breads. Makes 1 1/2 cups.

CUCUMBER DILL DIP OR SAUCE

1	**small cucumber,** peeled, seeded, and chopped
1/2 cup	**Powdered Milk Yogurt** (page 12)
2 teaspoons	**snipped fresh dill or 1/2 teaspoon dried dill or dill weed**
1 teaspoon	**skim milk or water**
1/2 teaspoon	**sugar**
1/2 teaspoon	**prepared yellow mustard**
	pinch salt
	pinch white or black pepper

Mix all ingredients together in a small bowl and refrigerate until ready to use. Serve as a dip for vegetables or chips, or use as a sauce for fish, beef, or chicken. Makes approximately 1 1/2 cups.

SPINACH ARTICHOKE DIP

1 bag (2 pounds)	**frozen spinach**
1 can (14 ounces)	**artichoke hearts**
2 cups	**Powdered Milk Baker's Cheese** (page 22) **or Powdered Milk Yogurt Cream Cheese** (page 14)
2 cups	**grated Powdered Milk Mozzarella Cheese** (page 25)
1 1/2 to 2 cups	**grated Parmesan cheese**
2 teaspoons	**minced garlic**
	salt and pepper, to taste

Combine all ingredients in a 2-quart slow cooker and cook on low for 2–3 hours, stirring often. Serve with tortilla chips or sliced baguettes. Makes 6 cups.

LAYERED MEXICAN DIP

2 cups	**Powdered Milk Yogurt** (page 12)
1/2 teaspoon	**taco seasoning mix**
1 cup	**refried beans or mashed beans**
1 cup	**salsa,** divided
1 cup	**grated cheddar cheese**
1 cup	**shredded lettuce**
1 cup	**sliced black or green olives**

Combine the yogurt and seasoning mix together in a small bowl.

In an 8 x 11-inch casserole dish, mix the beans and 1/3 cup salsa together and spread evenly over bottom. Layer the seasoned yogurt, remaining salsa, cheese, lettuce, and olives on top in that order. Cover and chill until ready to use. Makes 8–10 servings.

VARIATION: Omit the salsa and lettuce and add 1 cup guacamole, chopped tomatoes, and chopped green onions.

SALMON CHEESE SPREAD

1 cup	**Powdered Milk Baker's Cheese** (page 22) **or Powdered Milk Yogurt Cream Cheese** (page 14)
1 package (4 ounces)	**Bumble Bee Lemon-Dill Pink Salmon**
1/4 cup	**fresh spinach**
	lime juice, to taste
	garlic, to taste
	salt, to taste

Place all ingredients in a blender or food processor and mix until well combined. Chill in refrigerator 2–3 hours before serving. Serve with crackers, vegetables, or sliced baguette. Makes 1 1/2 cups.

SHRIMP SPREAD

1/3 cup	**Powdered Milk Baker's Cheese** (page 22) **or Powdered Milk Yogurt Cream Cheese** (page 14)
1 can (4.5 ounces)	**broken shrimp pieces or 1/2 cup frozen shrimp,** thawed and chopped
2 tablespoons	**mayonnaise**
1 tablespoon	**lemon juice**
1/4 teaspoon	**dill weed**
1 sprig	**parsley,** stem removed

Place all ingredients in a blender or food processor and mix until well combined. Chill in refrigerator 2–3 hours before serving. Serve with crackers, sliced baguette, or snack rye bread. Makes 1 cup.

FRESH CHEESE WITH CHIVES

2 cups	**Powdered Milk Baker's Cheese** (page 22) **or Powdered Milk Yogurt Cream Cheese** (page 14)
1 tablespoon	**chopped fresh parsley or cilantro**
1 tablespoon	**chopped fresh chives**
1 tablespoon	**fresh lemon or lime zest**
1 tablespoon	**minced fresh garlic**
1 teaspoon	**sea salt**

Place all ingredients in a blender or food processor and mix until well combined. Chill in refrigerator 2–3 hours before serving. Serve with bagels or crackers. Makes 2 cups.

NOTE: If you would like it softer, add 1 tablespoon of lemon or lime juice.

CINNAMON SPREAD

½ cup	**Powdered Milk Baker's Cheese** (page 22) **or Powdered Milk Yogurt Cream Cheese** (page 14)
1 to 2 tablespoons	**honey**
¼ teaspoon	**ground cinnamon**

Place all ingredients in a small bowl and mix until well combined. Serve with bagels, toast, or scones. Makes ½ cup.

NOTE: You can make any kind of sweet spread by using cream cheese with jam, preserves, or compote. Use pineapple or fresh fruit with a sweetener. Anything can be mixed in to achieve the taste you'd like. You can even add ground nuts.

CHEESE BALL

2 cups	**Powdered Milk Baker's Cheese** (page 22) **or Powdered Milk Yogurt Cream Cheese** (page 14)
1 bottle (5 ounces)	**Kraft Old English Cheese Spread**
1 can (6.75 ounces)	**chopped ham**
1 teaspoon	**lemon juice**
1/4 teaspoon	**garlic salt or garlic powder**
1 to 2 teaspoons	**minced onion or chives,** fresh or dried
1/4 teaspoon	**Worcestershire sauce**
1/2 cup	**chopped walnuts,** optional
	several sprigs parsley, chopped, optional

Place all ingredients, except nuts and parsley, in a blender or food processor and mix until well combined. Form into a ball and roll in walnuts and/or parsley. Chill in refrigerator 2–3 hours before serving. Serve with bagels or crackers. Makes 1 cheese ball.

BUTTERMILK MAPLE SYRUP

1/2 cup	**butter**
1 cup	**sugar**
1 cup	**Powdered Milk Buttermilk** (page 15)
1 tablespoon	**corn syrup**
1 tablespoon	**maple extract**
1/2 teaspoon	**baking soda**

Place all ingredients except baking soda in a large saucepan and bring to a boil, stirring constantly. Boil 1 minute, remove from heat, and add baking soda, stirring until thoroughly mixed. It will foam at this point. Serve over pancakes, French toast, waffles, or even ice cream. When you reheat any leftover syrup, it will expand, so warm it in a container double the amount of liquid. Makes 3 cups.

NOTE: Recipe courtesy of Ashley Alexander.

SAUCES, SOUPS & SALADS

ALLEMANDE SAUCE

1 1/4 cups	**chicken broth**
1	**egg**
1/4 cup	**powdered milk**
2 tablespoons	**flour**
1/4 teaspoon	**salt**
3 tablespoons	**butter**
1 tablespoon	**lemon juice**

Pour the broth in a blender and turn on low, add the egg, powdered milk, flour, and salt. Blend just until mixed. Pour in a small saucepan, bring to a boil, and cook for 1 minute, stirring constantly.* Remove from stove, add butter and lemon juice, and stir until blended.

Serve as a sauce over fish or chicken, or use in place of canned creamed soups in recipes. Makes 2 cups.

*If desired, add any cooked meats, fish, or vegetables at this point to serve over noodles or rice.

ALFREDO SAUCE

1/2 cup	**butter**
1/2 cup	**flour**
3 cups	**chicken broth**
3 cups	**Powdered Milk Evaporated Milk** (page 17)
1/2 teaspoon	**salt**
4 cloves	**garlic,** crushed
3 cups	**grated Parmesan cheese**

In a large saucepan, melt butter and add flour; stir and cook 1 minute. Add broth, stir and cook until thickened. Add milk, salt, and garlic and bring to a boil. Sprinkle in the cheese while stirring until smooth.* Serve the sauce over meats, vegetables, noodles, or rice. Makes 8 cups.

*You can add any cooked meats, fish, or vegetables at this point.

NOTE: Recipe courtesy of Tracey Lou Mullen.

THIN, MEDIUM, AND THICK WHITE SAUCE

Thin:

1 cup	**water**
3 tablespoons	**powdered milk**
1 tablespoon	**butter**
1 tablespoon	**flour**
1/4 teaspoon	**salt**
	dash white pepper

Medium:

1 cup	**water**
3 tablespoons	**powdered milk**
2 tablespoons	**butter**
2 tablespoons	**flour**
1/4 teaspoon	**salt**
	dash white pepper

Thick:

1 cup	**water**
3 tablespoons	**powdered milk**
3 tablespoons	**butter**
4 tablespoons	**flour**
1/4 teaspoon	**salt**
	dash white pepper

Place water in a blender, turn on low, and add powdered milk. Blend until mixed.

Melt butter in a small saucepan over medium-low heat. Blend in flour, salt and pepper and cook, stirring constantly until bubbly then add the milk all at once. Stir constantly while cooking until mixture thickens and bubbles. Makes 1 cup.

VARIATIONS: This sauce can be used as a base for all kinds of sauces and can be used instead of creamed canned soups.

Cheese: Add 1 cup of grated cheese.

Cream of Chicken: Use chicken broth instead of water, or juice drained off of canned chicken. Add a little of the canned or leftover chicken finely ground or chopped with a dash of onion powder.

Cream of Mushroom: Use beef broth instead of water. Add diced mushrooms, canned or fresh, with a dash of garlic powder.

Mexican: Use chicken broth instead of water and 1/2 teaspoon chili powder.

Use 1/2 teaspoon for powders and 1 teaspoon for fresh of any spice or herb to change the flavors, like curry powder or turmeric, dill, or cilantro. Use broths or bouillons in place of the water. Add cooked meats and vegetables, and serve over potatoes, rice, noodles, or couscous. You can make so many different dishes with this basic recipe.

CREAMED EGGS

3 cups	**water**
1/2 cup plus 1 tablespoon	**powdered milk**
6 tablespoons	**butter**
6 tablespoons	**flour**
3/4 teaspoon	**seasoned salt**
6	**hard-boiled eggs,** peeled and chopped
1/4 to 1/2 cup	**grated cheese,** of choice, optional
	cooked sausage, bacon, or ham, to taste, optional
	dash of Tabasco Sauce, optional
1/4 teaspoon	**cumin or seasonings,** of choice

Pour the water into a blender, turn on low, add the powdered milk, and blend until just mixed.

Melt butter in a large saucepan. Add flour and salt. Stir with a whisk until bubbly. Add the milk and stir until thickened. Add chopped eggs and remaining ingredients, if using. Cook 2–3 minutes. Serve over biscuits or toast. Makes 5–6 cups.

BLACK BEAN SOUP

1	**small onion,** chopped
1 tablespoon	**cumin**
1 tablespoon	**cooking oil**
3 cans (16 ounces each)	**black beans,** with liquid, divided
1 can (14 ounces)	**chicken broth**
3 cups	**chunky salsa**
1	**lime,** juiced
	Powdered Milk Yogurt (page 12) **or Powdered Milk Sour Cream** (page 23)

In a large soup pot, cook onion and cumin in oil until translucent.

In a blender, puree 2 cans of beans with the broth and add to the onions with remaining can of beans, salsa, and lime juice. Heat to a boil, reduce to low and simmer for 30 minutes. Serve with a dollop of yogurt or sour cream on top. Makes 6 servings.

NOTE: Recipe courtesy of Amy Newby.

RICH POTATO SOUP

2 cups	**diced potatoes**
1 cup	**diced celery**
1 cup	**diced onion**
1/3 cup	**flour**
4 teaspoons	**chicken bouillon granules**
1 can (15 ounces)	**corn,** drained
1/4 to 1/2 cup	**butter,** softened
	crumbled bacon or diced cooked ham, to taste
	salt and pepper, to taste
3/4 cup	**Powdered Milk Yogurt** (page 12) **or Powdered Milk Sour Cream** (page 23)

In a large soup pot, add potatoes, celery, and onion with enough water to cover, and cook until tender.

In a small bowl, add flour, bouillon, corn, butter, and bacon and mix until well combined. Add to potatoes and continue cooking until thickened, stirring constantly. If too thick, add milk or water to desired consistency. Add salt and pepper and yogurt or sour cream. Stir in until heated through. Makes 6 servings.

NOTE: Recipe courtesy of Amy Newby.

SCALLOPED POTATO SOUP

2 tablespoons	**butter**
1	**onion,** diced
2 cloves	**garlic,** minced
2	**carrots,** diced
4	**large potatoes,** diced
1/2 to 1 pound	**cooked ham,** cubed
1/2 cup	**water**
1 tablespoon	**vegetable or chicken bouillon granules**
4 cups	**water,** divided
1 3/4 cups	**powdered milk**
1/4 cup	**flour**
1/2 pound	**cheddar cheese,** grated or cubed
1/4 cup	**chopped fresh parsley**
	salt and pepper, to taste

In a Dutch oven or large heavy-bottom stock pot on medium-low heat, melt butter then add onion, garlic, carrots, and potatoes and saute until onions are translucent. Add ham and cook for 2–3 minutes. Add 1/2 cup water and bouillon; cover and steam until vegetables are tender.

Add 2 cups of water to a blender, turn on low, and add powdered milk and flour and blend on low just until mixed. Add milk and the rest of the water to the vegetables. Cook until just starting to bubble then add cheese, parsley, salt and pepper. Cook until the cheese has melted and soup has thickened, but do not boil. Makes 6 servings.

BROCCOLI-CHEDDAR SOUP

3 cups	**chicken broth**
1/2 to 1	**onion,** chopped
4 cups	**chopped broccoli**
	dash garlic powder
1/2 teaspoon	**thyme**
2	**bay leaves**
1/4 cup	**butter**
1/4 cup	**flour**
1/2 teaspoon	**salt**
	dash pepper
2 cups	**prepared Powdered Milk** (2 cups water mixed with 1/2 cup powdered milk)
2 cups	**grated cheddar cheese**

In a large soup pot, add broth, onion, broccoli, garlic power, thyme, and bay leaves. Bring to a boil, reduce heat, and simmer 10 minutes or until vegetables are tender.

Remove bay leaves, and pour mixture into a blender or food processor, or use an immersion blender, if available, being careful with hot liquid. Blend or pulse until smooth, about 1 minute. Set aside.

Melt the butter in the soup pot and whisk in flour, salt, and pepper to make a paste. Add milk and stir constantly until thickened. Add cheese and stir until blended. Add broccoli mixture and cook until heated through. Thin with more broth to desired consistency, if needed. Makes 6 servings.

CORN CHOWDER

1 tablespoon	**cooking oil**
1/2 cup	**chopped onion**
1/2 cup	**chopped celery**
4 cups	**water,** divided
2 cups	**diced or shredded potatoes**
3/4 cup	**powdered milk**
2 tablespoons	**flour**
1 teaspoon	**salt**
	pepper, to taste
1 can (15 ounces)	**cream-style corn**
1/2 pound	**bacon,** cooked and crumbled

Heat oil in a large soup pot and add onion and celery; saute until translucent. Add 3 cups water and potatoes and simmer until tender.

In blender, add remaining water, powdered milk, flour, salt, and pepper and blend until just mixed. Add to potatoes and cook until it just starts to thicken. Add corn and bacon and continue cooking until corn is heated through. Makes 4–6 servings.

SHRIMP AND CLAM CHOWDER

1 cup	**chopped onion**
1 cup	**chopped celery**
1 cup	**chopped carrots**
1 cup	**chopped potato**
1 teaspoon	**salt**
1/2 teaspoon	**sugar**
1/4 teaspoon	**pepper**
1/4 teaspoon	**seasoning salt**
1 can (6 ounces)	**minced clams,** drained, juice reserved
1 cup	**chopped shrimp**
4 cups	**water**
1 1/2 cups	**powdered milk**
3/4 cup	**butter**
3/4 cup	**flour**
	grated cheese, of choice
	croutons

In a large soup pot, add onion, celery, carrots, potato, seasonings, and clam juice with enough water to cover; cook until vegetables are tender. Add clams and shrimp.

In a blender, add water and powdered milk and blend on low until just mixed.

In a large saucepan, melt butter and stir in flour to make a paste; cook for 2 minutes. Add milk and cook until thickened, stirring constantly. Add to vegetables and stir to heat through. Serve topped with grated cheese or croutons. Makes 6 servings.

APPLE SALAD

1/2 cup	**Powdered Milk Yogurt** (page 12)
1 tablespoon	**agave nectar or honey**
1/4 teaspoon	**almond, lemon, or vanilla extract**
1	**apple,** cored and chopped
2 tablespoons	**chopped walnuts**

In a small bowl add yogurt, nectar, and extract; mix to combine. Add apple and walnuts and toss to coat. Makes 1–2 servings.

CRANBERRY WALDORF SALAD

1 1/2 cups	**chopped cranberries,** fresh or frozen
1 cup	**chopped red apple**
1 cup	**chopped celery**
1 cup	**seedless green grapes**
1/3 cup	**raisins**
1/4 cup	**chopped walnuts**
2 tablespoons	**sugar or sweetener,** of choice
1/2 teaspoon	**vanilla**
1 cup	**Powdered Milk Yogurt** (page 12)
1/4 teaspoon	**ground cinnamon**

In a large bowl, mix together cranberries, apple, celery, grapes, raisins, walnuts, and sugar. In a small bowl, add vanilla to yogurt, mixing well to combine. Add yogurt and cinnamon to fruit and toss to coat. Makes 5–6 servings.

MAIN DISHES

STROGANOFF

1 pound	**ground or cubed beef**
1/2 cup	**chopped onion**
1/4 cup	**chopped mushrooms**
1/4 cup	**butter or cooking oil**
1/4 cup	**flour**
1/4 teaspoon	**garlic powder**
1 teaspoon	**paprika**
2 1/2 cups	**beef broth**
1 tablespoon	**Worcestershire sauce**
2 cups	**Powdered Milk Yogurt Sour Cream** (page 13) **or Powdered Milk Yogurt** (page 12)
	cooked noodles or rice

In a large frying pan, saute beef, onions, and mushrooms in butter. Add flour, garlic powder, and paprika and stir to combine. Add broth and stir until smooth and thickened. Add Worcestershire sauce and sour cream. Heat through; do not bring to a boil. Serve over noodles or rice. Makes 6–8 servings.

NOTE: Recipe courtesy of Tracey Lou Mullen.

EASY TACO PIE

1 pound	**ground turkey**
1	**medium onion,** chopped
1 package (1.25 ounces)	**taco seasoning mix**
1 can (15 ounces)	**pinto or black beans,** with liquid
1 can (4 ounces)	**green chiles**
1/2 cup	**Homemade Biscuit Mix** (page 44)
3 tablespoons	**powdered milk**
1 cup	**water**
2	**eggs**
1/2 cup	**grated Mexican blend cheese**
1	**tomato,** chopped
	shredded lettuce
	sliced green onions, optional

Preheat oven to 400 degrees. Prepare a glass pie plate with nonstick cooking spray.

In a large frying pan, brown turkey and onion until meat is cooked through; drain excess fat. Add seasoning mix and beans, mixing well. Spread on bottom of pie plate and cover with green chiles.

In a medium bowl, combine the biscuit mix and powdered milk. Add water and eggs and mix until well blended. Pour over mixture in pie plate and bake for 25 minutes. Top with cheese and tomato and place back in the oven for 2–3 minutes longer, or until cheese is melted. Remove from oven and let stand 5 minutes before serving. Top with shredded lettuce and green onions. Makes 4–6 servings.

NOTE: Recipe courtesy of Amy Newby.

BEEFY ENCHILADAS

1 pound	**ground beef**
1/2 cup	**chopped onion**
1 can (16 ounces)	**refried beans**
1/2 teaspoon	**salt**
1/4 teaspoon	**pepper**
10	**corn tortillas,** softened
1 can (14.5 ounces)	**diced tomatoes**

Sauce:

4 tablespoons	**butter**
1/4 cup	**flour**
6 tablespoons	**powdered milk**
2 cups	**water**
1 can (10 ounces)	**red enchilada sauce**
1 1/2 cups	**grated Mexican blend cheese**
3/4 cup	**sliced olives**

Preheat oven to 350 degrees.

In a large frying pan, brown the beef and onion until meat is cooked through; drain excess fat. Stir in beans, salt, and pepper. Place 1/3 cup of mixture and a spoonful of tomatoes in each tortilla and roll. Place seam side down in a 9 x 13-inch pan that has been prepared with nonstick cooking spray.

For sauce, melt butter in a large saucepan and stir in flour until smooth. Mix powdered milk and water in blender and add to saucepan along with enchilada sauce; cook and stir until smooth. Add cheese and olives and continue cooking over medium-high heat until cheese melts and sauce starts to bubble. Pour over enchiladas, cover, and bake for 30 minutes. Makes 10 enchiladas

NOTE: Recipe courtesy of Amy Newby.

CHICKEN ENCHILADAS

1 can (10.5 ounces)	**condensed cream of chicken soup**
1/2 cup	**Powdered Milk Yogurt** (page 12) **or Powdered Milk Yogurt Sour Cream** (page 13)
2 tablespoons	**butter**
1/2 cup	**chopped onion**
1/2 to 1 teaspoon	**chili powder**
2 cups	**diced cooked chicken**
1 can (4 ounces)	**chopped green chiles**
8 to 10 (8-inch)	**flour tortillas**
1 cup	**grated cheddar cheese**

Preheat oven to 375 degrees.

In a small bowl, mix together soup and yogurt; set aside.

In a large frying pan, melt butter and add onion and chili powder. Saute until onion is translucent. Stir in chicken, chiles, and 2 tablespoons soup mixture; heat through.

Spread a little of the soup mixture in the bottom of a 9 x 13-inch pan. Spoon about 1/4 cup of meat mixture over each tortilla and roll, placing seam side down in pan. Pour soup mixture over tortillas and sprinkle with cheese. Cover and bake, approximately 20 minutes, or until sauce starts to bubble. Makes 8–10 enchiladas.

NOTE: Recipe courtesy of Ashley Alexander.

BAKED CHICKEN TAQUITOS

1/2 cup	**Powdered Milk Day Cheese** (page 24) **or Powdered Milk Cottage Cheese** (page 21)
2 cups	**cooked shredded chicken**
1 cup	**grated Mexican blend cheese or pepper jack cheese**
1/4 cup	**green salsa**
1 tablespoon	**lime juice**
1/2 teaspoon	**cumin**
1/2 teaspoon	**chili powder**
1/2 teaspoon	**onion powder**
1/2 teaspoon	**minced garlic**
3 tablespoons	**chopped cilantro**
2 tablespoons	**chopped green onion**
12 to 14 (6-inch)	**corn or flour tortillas** (as fresh as possible)
2 tablespoons	**cooking oil**
	kosher salt

Preheat oven to 425 degrees. Prepare a baking sheet with nonstick cooking spray.

In a large bowl, mix together all ingredients except tortillas, oil, and salt.

Wrap 3–4 tortillas in damp paper towels and heat in microwave for 30 seconds to make soft and pliable.

Spread 2–3 tablespoons of chicken mixture on each tortilla, keeping it about a 1/2 inch from the edge. Roll up and place seam side down on baking sheet. Brush top of tortillas with oil and sprinkle lightly with salt. Bake 15–20 minutes, or until crisp and the ends start to turn golden brown. Makes 12–14 taquitos.

QUICK CHICKEN ALFREDO

2	**boneless, skinless chicken breasts,** sliced or cubed
1 tablespoon	**minced garlic**
2 tablespoons	**olive oil**
1/2 cup	**chicken broth**
1 can (10.5 ounces)	**condensed cream of chicken or mushroom soup**
1 cup	**frozen peas or vegetable,** of choice, optional
1 cup	**Powdered Milk Yogurt** (page 12)
	cooked noodles or rice

In a large frying pan, saute chicken and garlic in oil over medium heat until chicken is cooked through. Stir in broth, soup, and peas. Cook until peas are heated and add yogurt. Heat through, but do not let come to a boil. Serve over noodles or rice. Makes 4–6 servings.

THREE-CHEESE CHICKEN LASAGNA

1/2 cup	**chopped onion**
3 tablespoons	**butter**
1 can (10.5 ounces)	**condensed cream of chicken soup**
1/3 cup	**prepared Powdered Milk** (1/3 cup water plus 1 tablespoon powdered milk)
1 1/2 cups	**Powdered Milk Cottage Cheese** (page 21)
1/2 cup	**grated Monterey Jack cheese**
1/2 teaspoon	**sweet basil**
3 cups	**cubed cooked chicken**
2 cups	**grated cheddar cheese**
1 package (8 ounces)	**lasagna noodles,** cooked

Preheat oven to 350 degrees.

In a large frying pan, saute onion in butter until translucent. Mix in remaining ingredients except cheddar cheese and noodles.

Place 1/2 of the noodles in the bottom of a 9 x 13-inch pan and layer 1/2 of the chicken mixture and 1/2 of the cheddar cheese over noodles. Repeat layer. Cover and bake for 45 minutes. Let set for 5–10 minutes before cutting and serving. Makes 12–16 servings.

NOTE: Recipe courtesy of Tracey Lou Mullen.

CHICKEN POT PIE

2 cups	**chicken broth,** divided
1/2 to 1 cup	**chopped onion**
1 1/2 to 2 cups	**diced potatoes**
2 cups	**assorted fresh or frozen vegetables,** of choice (carrots, peas, squash, mushrooms, celery, bell peppers, or corn)
1/4 teaspoon	**thyme,** or to taste
1 cup	**water**
1/4 cup	**cornstarch**
3 tablespoons	**powdered milk**
1 teaspoon	**Dijon mustard**
2 cups	**diced cooked chicken or turkey**
	salt and pepper, to taste
1 (9-inch)	**premade pie crust or Jiffy or Bisquick crust**

Preheat oven to 400 degrees.

In a large saucepan, bring 1 cup broth to boil and add onion. Cook 3 minutes and add remaining broth, vegetables, and thyme. Cook until vegetables are tender.

Pour water in a blender, turn on low, and add the cornstarch, powdered milk, and mustard. Mix until blended, add to the vegetables, and cook 5 minutes. Add chicken, salt, and pepper. Pour mixture into a deep 9-inch casserole dish or pie plate. Cover with uncooked pie crust or Jiffy or Bisquick crust (2 cups mix, 1/2 cup milk, mix and roll out). Cut slits in the top to vent and bake for 20 minutes, or until crust starts to turn golden brown. Makes 4–6 servings.

NOTE: Recipe courtesy of Amy Newby.

CHICKEN LIK-OOP

1/2 pound	**bacon,** chopped
2 cups	**chopped or sliced cooked chicken**
1/2 cup	**chicken broth**
3 cups	**Powdered Milk Evaporated Milk** (page 17)
1/2 teaspoon	**seasoning salt**
	cooked rice

In a large frying pan, fry bacon until crisp; drain bacon grease. Add remaining ingredients and simmer 10 minutes. Serve over cooked rice. Makes 4–5 servings.

NOTE: Recipe courtesy of Tracey Lou Mullen

LASAGNA

1 pound	**ground Italian sausage**
1 clove	**garlic,** minced
1 tablespoon	**basil**
2 cans (16 ounces each)	**crushed tomatoes**
2	**eggs**
3 cups	**Powdered Milk Cottage Cheese** (page 21)
1/2 cup	**grated Parmesan cheese**
2 tablespoons	**parsley flakes**
1/2 teaspoon	**salt**
1 package (16 ounces)	**lasagna noodles,** cooked
2 cups	**grated Powdered Milk Mozzarella Cheese** (page 25)
1 can (6 ounces)	**tomato sauce**

Preheat oven to 375 degrees.

In a large frying pan, brown sausage until cooked through; drain excess fat. Add garlic, basil, and tomatoes. Simmer for 5–10 minutes.

In a large bowl, beat eggs and add cottage cheese, Parmesan, parsley, and salt. In a 9 x 13-inch pan, layer 1/2 the noodles, and top with 1/2 the cottage cheese filling, 1/2 the meat sauce, and 1/2 the mozzarella. Repeat layers. Pour tomato sauce over top, cover with foil, and bake for 45 minutes. Let rest 5–10 minutes before cutting. Makes 12–16 servings.

NOTE: Recipe courtesy of Tracey Lou Mullen.

FAUX FETTUCCINE

1 package (8 ounces)	**fettuccine noodles**
1/2 cup	**frozen peas**
1/2 cup	**grated carrots**
3 tablespoons	**butter**
3/4 cup	**Parmesan cheese**
1 cup	**Powdered Milk Yogurt** (page 12)
1 teaspoon	**parsley flakes**
1/4 teaspoon	**salt**
	dash pepper

In a large saucepan, cook fettuccine according to package directions. About 3 minutes before noodles are finished cooking, add peas and carrots. Finish cooking, drain, and return to pan. Add butter and mix until melted.

In a medium bowl, combine cheese, yogurt, parsley, salt, and pepper. Add to noodle mixture and toss until noodles are coated. Serve hot. Makes 4–6 servings.

NOTE: Recipe courtesy of Utah State University Weber Extension.

CHEESY MEATBALL SKILLET

1 pound	**ground turkey**
10	**saltine crackers,** crushed
1/4 cup	**Zesty Italian Salad Dressing**
1 cup	**water**
2	**beef bouillon cubes**
1 cup	**Powdered Milk Yogurt** (page 12) **or Powdered Milk Yogurt Sour Cream** (page 13)
1 to 2 cups	**grated cheddar cheese**
	cooked pasta or rice

Preheat oven to 375 degrees.

In a medium bowl, combine turkey, crackers, and dressing; shape into 1-inch balls. Place meatballs in an 8 x 8-inch pan and bake for 30–35 minutes, or until cooked through.

In a large saucepan, add the water, bouillon, and cooked meatballs; simmer for 5 minutes. Stir in yogurt and cook 30 seconds until heated through, stirring constantly. Remove from heat, add cheese, cover, and let melt for about 5 minutes. Serve over pasta or rice. Makes 6 servings.

NOTE: Recipe courtesy of Amy Newby.

TUNA CRUNCH PIE

1 1/2 cups	**flour**
1 1/2 cups	**grated cheddar cheese,** divided
1 teaspoon	**salt**
1 teaspoon	**paprika**
1/2 cup	**butter**
2 cans (7 ounces each)	**tuna,** drained
3	**eggs**
1 cup	**Powdered Milk Baker's Cheese** (page 22) **or Powdered Milk Yogurt** (page 12)
1/4 cup	**mayonnaise**
1/4 teaspoon	**onion powder**
1/4 teaspoon	**dried dill weed**
2 drops	**hot pepper sauce**

Preheat oven to 400 degrees.

In a medium bowl, combine flour, 1 cup cheese, salt, paprika, and butter; mix until it resembles coarse crumbs. Reserve 1 cup mixture for topping and press the rest into the bottom of a 10-inch pie dish that has been prepared with nonstick cooking spray. Sprinkle tuna over top of crust.

In a medium bowl, beat the eggs and mix in remaining ingredients; pour over top of tuna. Sprinkle with reserved crumb mixture and bake for 35–40 minutes. Cool for 10 minutes before serving. Makes 6 servings.

NOTE: Recipe courtesy of Tracey Lou Mullen.

GARDEN-STUFFED BAKED POTATOES

6	**medium baking potatoes**
1/4 cup	**chopped onion**
1/2 cup	**chopped broccoli or zucchini**
1/2 cup	**chopped ham or bacon crumbles**
1 tablespoon	**cooking oil**
1/2 cup	**Powdered Milk Cottage Cheese** (page 21)
1/4 cup	**butter,** softened
2 to 4 tablespoons	**Ranch Salad Dressing**
1/4 cup	**grated cheddar cheese**
	salt and pepper, to taste

Preheat oven to 400 degrees.

Puncture the potatoes several times on each side and place in the microwave. Cook 6–7 minutes, turn over, and cook 6–7 minutes more.

While potatoes are cooking, saute onion, broccoli, and ham in oil until onion is translucent. Mix together remaining ingredients in a large bowl and add the broccoli mixture.

When potatoes are finished cooking, slice a wedge out of the tops and set aside. Scoop out the insides of the potatoes and add to the broccoli mixture, mix together, and season to taste. Stuff the mixture back into the potato shells and place on a baking sheet. Brush the potato top wedges with a little oil or butter and sprinkle with coarse salt, place skin side up on baking sheet. Bake for 10–15 minutes. Makes 6 servings.

NOTE: Recipe courtesy of Amy Newby.

HASH-BROWN SAUSAGE BAKE

1 bag (24 ounces)	**frozen hash-brown potatoes**
1/3 cup	**butter,** melted
1 teaspoon	**beef bouillon granules**
1 pound	**ground sausage, chopped ham, or bacon**
1/3 cup	**chopped onion**
5	**eggs**
1 cup	**Powdered Milk Cottage Cheese** (page 21)
1/2 cup	**grated cheddar cheese**

Preheat oven to 350 degrees.

Place hash browns in a 9 x 13-inch pan that has been prepared with nonstick cooking spray and drizzle butter over top. Sprinkle with bouillon. Bake, uncovered, for 25 minutes.

In a large frying pan, saute sausage and onion until sausage is cooked through. Drain excess fat.

In a medium bowl, beat eggs together and mix in cheeses until well combined. Add sausage to egg mixture and pour over hash browns. Bake, uncovered, for another 40 minutes. Makes 12–16 servings.

VARIATION: For a Southwest flavor use pepper jack cheese and 1 small can of green chiles.

NOTE: Recipe courtesy of Tracey Lou Mullen.

BREAKFAST OMELET CASSEROLE

2 cups	**water**
6 tablespoons	**powdered milk**
16	**eggs,** beaten
2 cups	**Powdered Milk Mozzarella Cheese** (page 25)
2 cups	**grated cheddar cheese**
1/2 cup	**sliced green onions or chives**
1/2 teaspoon	**garlic salt**
1/2 teaspoon	**onion salt**
1 cup	**diced ham or cooked sausage**

Preheat oven to 325 degrees.

Pour water in a blender and turn on low, add powdered milk, and blend just until mixed.

Add milk to remaining ingredients in a large bowl and mix until well combined. Pour into a 9 x 13-inch pan that has been prepared with nonstick cooking spray and bake for 40–45 minutes. Makes 12–16 servings.

NOTE: Recipe courtesy of Amy Newby.

QUICHE A LA LORRAINE

1 (8-inch)	**premade pie crust**
1/2 pound	**bacon,** chopped, fried, and drained
1/2 cup	**grated Gruyere cheese or Swiss or provolone cheese**
4	**eggs**
2 cups	**water**
6 tablespoons	**powdered milk**
1/2 teaspoon	**salt**
	pinch pepper

Preheat oven to 375 degrees.

Fit pie crust into an 8-inch quiche dish or pie plate, layering bacon and cheese on bottom. Place eggs and water in a blender and turn on low, adding the powdered milk, salt, and pepper. Mix just until blended. Pour over bacon and cheese. Bake for 35–40 minutes, or until a knife inserted in the center comes out clean. Cool 10 minutes before cutting. Makes 6 servings.

NOTE: Recipe courtesy of Tracey Lou Mullen.

DESSERTS & TREATS

CREPES

2 to 3	**eggs**
1 1/2 cups	**flour**
6 tablespoons	**powdered milk**
1/4 teaspoon	**salt**
1 cup	**water**
1 cup	**Powdered Milk Buttermilk** (page 15)
3 tablespoons	**butter,** melted
1/2 teaspoon	**vanilla, lemon, almond, or orange extract,** optional*
3 tablespoons	**sugar,** optional*

In a medium bowl, beat eggs and whisk in flour, powdered milk, and salt. Gradually add water, buttermilk, butter, extract, and sugar, if using. Beat until smooth.

Prepare a small frying pan with nonstick cooking spray and heat on medium low. Pour 1/4 cup of batter in bottom of pan and swirl to coat. Cook for 1 minute until top appears dry. Flip crepe and cook an additional 30 seconds. Spray pan again every 3–4 crepes. If using a crepe maker, follow maker's instructions. Use crepes with filling, of choice. Makes 12 crepes.

*Use the flavoring and sugar when making crepes for desserts and sweet fillings. Do not add when making crepes for egg or meat fillings.

BAKED CHEESECAKE

Crust:

	1 1/2 cups	**graham cracker crumbs**
	1/4 cup	**sugar**
	1/3 cup	**butter,** softened

Filling:

	3 cups	**Powdered Milk Yogurt Cream Cheese** (page 14) **or Powdered Milk Baker's Cheese** (page 22)
	1 1/4 cups	**sugar**
	4	**eggs**
	2 teaspoons	**vanilla**
	2 tablespoons	**cornstarch**

Topping:

	1 cup	**Powdered Milk Yogurt Sour Cream** (page 13)
	3 tablespoons	**sugar**
	1 teaspoon	**vanilla**

Preheat oven to 350 degrees. In a small bowl, combine crumbs, sugar, and butter. Spread in the bottom of a 9-inch springform pan and pat firmly and evenly. Chill.

In a blender, combine filling ingredients and process until smooth. Pour into prepared crust and bake for 40 minutes. When the edges of the cake are set and lightly browned, but the center remains unset, whisk together the topping ingredients in a small bowl and pour over the top and edges of the cheesecake. Bake another 7–10 minutes, or until the topping bubbles around the edges. Chill well before unmolding and cutting. Makes 8–10 servings.

EASY CHEESECAKE

Crust:

8	**whole graham crackers,** crushed
3 tablespoons	**sugar**
6 tablespoons	**butter,** melted

Filling:

1/2 cup	**warm water**
3/4 cup	**powdered milk**
3/4 cup	**sugar**
1/4 cup	**lemon juice or orange juice**
1 teaspoon	**vanilla**
1 cup	**Powdered Milk Yogurt Cream Cheese** (page 14) **or Powdered Milk Baker's Cheese** (page 22)

Preheat oven to 400 degrees.

In a small bowl, combine crackers, sugar, and butter. Spread in the bottom of a 9-inch springform pan and pat firmly and evenly. Optional: Bake for 10 minutes, remove from oven, and let cool if you would like a crunchier crust.

Pour water in a blender and turn on to low. Add remaining filling ingredients and blend until just mixed. Pour into graham cracker crust. Chill in refrigerator at least 15 minutes before serving. Makes 8–10 servings.

YOGURT STREUSEL COFFEE CAKE

1/2 cup	**butter**
1 cup	**sugar**
2	**eggs**
1 cup	**Powdered Milk Yogurt** (page 12)
1 teaspoon	**almond extract**
2 cups	**flour**
1/2 teaspoon	**baking powder**
1/2 teaspoon	**salt**

Streusel:

1/2 cup	**brown sugar**
2 teaspoons	**flour**
2 teaspoons	**cinnamon**
1/2 cup	**chopped cashews or pecans**
2 tablespoons	**butter**

Preheat oven to 350 degrees. Grease and flour a Bundt pan.

In a large bowl, cream together butter, sugar, and eggs. Add yogurt and almond extract and beat for 1 minute. Add flour, baking powder, and salt and beat for 2 minutes. Pour into prepared pan.

Combine all streusel ingredients in a small bowl until mixed and damp. Pour along the top of the cake batter. Bake for 60 minutes. Cool in the pan for 5–10 minutes then turn out onto a cooling rack. Makes 16 servings.

LEMON YOGURT CAKE

1 cup	**butter,** softened
1 cup	**sugar**
4	**eggs**
1 tablespoon	**lemon zest**
1 teaspoon	**vanilla**
2 1/2 cups	**flour**
1 teaspoon	**baking powder**
1 teaspoon	**baking soda**
1/2 teaspoon	**salt**
1 cup	**Powdered Milk Yogurt** (page 12)
1 cup	**chopped almonds**

Sauce:

1/2 cup	**fresh lemon juice**
1/2 cup	**sugar**

Preheat oven to 350 degrees.

In a large bowl, cream together butter and sugar; beat in eggs, 1 at a time, until well blended. Add zest and vanilla.

Sift dry ingredients in a medium bowl and add alternately with yogurt to creamed mixture, beating well after each addition. Fold in almonds and pour into a 9-inch Bundt or tube pan that has been prepared with nonstick cooking spray and dusted with flour. Bake for 45–60 minutes. It is done when a toothpick inserted in the center of the cake comes out clean. Cool 5–10 minutes before removing from pan.

In a small saucepan, bring lemon juice and sugar to a boil, reduce heat, and simmer 5 minutes. Spoon over cake when ready to serve. Makes 8–10 servings.

CREAM CHEESE FROSTING

1/3 cup	**Powdered Milk Yogurt Cream Cheese** (page 14) **or Powdered Milk Baker's Cheese** (page 22)
1 tablespoon	**milk**
2 1/2 cups	**powdered sugar**
1/2 teaspoon	**vanilla or almond extract**

In a medium bowl, blend together cream cheese and milk. Mix well. Gradually add sugar and vanilla until well combined. Makes enough frosting for a 9 x 13-inch cake.

BASIC COOKIE MIX

9 cups	**flour**
3 cups	**powdered milk**
3 tablespoons	**baking powder**
1 tablespoon	**salt**
4 cups	**vegetable shortening**
4 cups	**sugar**

In a large bowl, sift together the flour, powdered milk, baking powder, and salt. Do this twice to incorporate well.

Beat the shortening to soften in the bowl of stand mixer. Gradually add the sugar, beating until creamy. Add the dry ingredients and blend well on low speed until crumbly. Store tightly covered at room temperature. It will keep for several weeks. Use this as the base for many different kinds of cookies. Makes about 14 dozen cookies.

NOTE: This was adapted from a similar item in *Deseret Recipes*.

OATMEAL COOKIES

1 cup	**raisins**
2/3 cup	**water**
2 cups	**Basic Cookie Mix** (page 102)
1 cup	**oatmeal**
2 tablespoons	**brown sugar**
1/2 teaspoon	**allspice**
1	**egg**
1 1/2	**teaspoons vanilla**
1/2 cup	**chopped nuts of choice,** optional

Preheat oven to 375 degrees.

In a small saucepan, bring raisins and water to a boil, reduce heat, and simmer for 5 minutes. Drain raisins, reserving 1/2 cup water.

Combine remaining ingredients, including reserved water, together in a large bowl and mix well. Stir in raisins. Drop by spoonfuls onto an ungreased baking sheet. Bake for 13–15 minutes. Makes 3 1/2–4 dozen (2-inch) cookies.

PEANUT BUTTER COOKIES

4 cups	**Basic Cookie Mix** (page 102)
1/4 cup	**brown sugar**
1/2 to 3/4 cup	**peanut butter**
1	**egg**
1 1/2 teaspoons	**vanilla**
1 tablespoon	**water**

Preheat oven to 375 degrees.

Combine all ingredients together in a large bowl and mix well. Roll dough into 1-inch balls, place on an ungreased baking sheet about 1 inch apart, and partially flatten with a fork. Bake for 10–12 minutes. Makes 7 dozen (1 1/2-inch) cookies.

LEMON DROP COOKIES

2 cups	**Basic Cookie Mix** (page 102)
1	**egg**
1 tablespoon	**lemon juice**
1 1/2 teaspoons	**lemon zest**

Preheat oven to 375 degrees.

Combine all ingredients together in a large bowl and mix well. Drop by spoonfuls onto an ungreased baking sheet. Bake for 13–15 minutes. Makes 2 1/2 dozen cookies.

CINNAMON COOKIES

2 1/2 cups	**Basic Cookie Mix** (page 102)
1 teaspoon	**vanilla**
1/2 cup	**sugar**
1	**egg**
1 1/2 teaspoons	**cinnamon**
1/2 cup	**finely chopped nuts,** of choice

Preheat oven to 375 degrees.

Combine cookie mix, vanilla, sugar, and egg in a large bowl; mix well. Combine cinnamon and nuts in a small bowl. Roll dough into 1 1/2-inch balls then roll in cinnamon and nut mixture. Place on an ungreased baking sheet and bake for 12–15 minutes. Makes 3 1/2–4 dozen (2-inch) cookies.

PECAN TASSIES

Dough:

    1 cup **flour**
    1/3 cup **Powdered Milk Yogurt Cream Cheese** (page 14) **or Powdered Milk Baker's Cheese** (page 22)
    1/2 cup **butter**

Filling:

    2 **eggs**
    1 cup **brown sugar**
    2 tablespoons **butter,** melted
    1 teaspoon **vanilla**
    1/2 cup **chopped pecans**

Preheat oven to 350 degrees.

In a medium bowl, add flour, cream cheese, and butter. Blend with a pastry cutter until dough starts to form and hold shape. Form into a ball, wrap with plastic wrap, and chill in refrigerator for 20–30 minutes.

In a medium bowl, add eggs, brown sugar, butter, vanilla, and pecans. Mix until well combined.

Prepare a muffin tin with nonstick cooking spray and then cover the bottom and sides of each cup with dough. Press into place. Fill each cup about half way with filling. Bake for 20–25 minutes, or until the filling is set. Makes 12 servings.

ROCKY ROAD CORNFLAKE COOKIES

2 cups	**cornflakes**
1/4 cup	**butter,** melted
1 cup	**chocolate chips**
1 cup	**shredded coconut**
1 cup	**chopped nuts,** of choice, optional
1 1/3 cups	**Powdered Milk Sweetened Condensed Milk** (page 18)

Preheat oven to 350 degrees.

Spread cornflakes in bottom of a 9 x 13-inch pan. Pour butter over cornflakes and sprinkle with chocolate chips, coconut, and nuts, if using. Pour condensed milk evenly over top. Bake for 15–17 minutes. Let cool and cut into squares. Makes 24 squares.

NOTE: Recipe courtesy of Amy Newby.

FRUIT SUPREME PIE

1 1/2 cups	**Powdered Milk Yogurt** (page 12), flavored with jam, of choice, or chopped fruit
3 1/2 cups	**Powdered Milk Whipped Topping** (page 20)
1 (8-inch)	**premade graham cracker crust**

Fold yogurt into whipped topping and pour into crust. Freeze until firm, about 2–4 hours. Makes 8–10 servings.

NOTE: Recipe courtesy of Tracey Lou Mullen.

PUDDING AND PIE FILLING

1 3/4 cups	**water,** divided*
1	**egg**
1/2 cup	**sugar**
3 tablespoons	**flour**
1 tablespoon	**cornstarch**
1/4 teaspoon	**salt**
1/3 cup	**powdered milk**
1 tablespoon	**butter**
1 teaspoon	**vanilla**

Bring 3/4 cup water to boil in a medium saucepan. Place the remaining water in a blender turned on low and add the egg, sugar, flour, cornstarch, salt, and powdered milk and mix until just blended. Add to the boiling water and cook on low or medium-low heat until mixture comes to a boil, stirring constantly. Cook 1 minute. Add butter and vanilla, remove from heat, and mix until smooth and blended. Serve hot or cold. Makes 2–2 1/2 cups.

*If making pie filling, use only 1 1/2 cups water.

VARIATIONS: Stir in any kind of fruit, nuts, marshmallows, or chocolate chips.

Chocolate: add 2 tablespoons of baking cocoa and 2 tablespoons sugar to dry ingredients.

Coconut: add $1/2$ cup shredded coconut with butter, and coconut extract instead of vanilla, if desired.

Butterscotch: use brown sugar instead of white and 1 more tablespoon of butter. Use butterscotch extract in place of vanilla, if desired.

Eggnog: use 2 eggs and rum flavoring instead of vanilla. Add a dash of nutmeg.

Maple nut: use brown sugar instead of white and maple flavoring instead of vanilla. Add chopped walnuts.

Banana: use smashed, chopped, or sliced bananas and banana flavoring.

Orange: use 2 tablespoons Tang Orange Drink with dry ingredients or use orange flavoring.

Fudgesicles or Pudding Pops: Pour the pudding into popsicle molds and freeze.

BREAD PUDDING

2 cups	**water**
1/4 cup plus 2 tablespoons	**powdered milk**
1 tablespoon	**butter**
1 1/2 cups	**soft bread cubes**
2	**eggs**
1/4 cup	**sugar**
1/4 teaspoon	**salt**
1/3 cup	**raisins or nuts**

Preheat oven to 350 degrees.

Add water to a blender, turn on low, and add powdered milk. Mix until just blended. Pour into a large saucepan and scald milk. Add butter and bread cubes and stir.

Beat the eggs in a medium bowl and add the sugar, salt, and raisins. Slowly add into the hot milk mixture, stirring constantly. Pour into a 9 x 9-inch or an 8 x 11-inch baking dish that has been prepared with nonstick cooking spray and set in a larger pan of hot water. Bake 1 hour or until set in the center. Serve warm. Makes 9–12 servings.

NOTE: Recipe courtesy of Utah State University Extension.

RICE PUDDING

2 cups	**water**
1/4 teaspoon	**salt**
1/4 cup	**uncooked rice**
1/4 cup	**raisins**
3/4 cup	**powdered milk**
1/4 cup	**sugar**
1 cup	**water,** divided
3/4 teaspoon	**vanilla**
	cinnamon or nutmeg, to taste

In a large saucepan, add water and salt and bring to a boil. Add rice, bring back to a boil, and lower heat to a simmer. Add raisins, cover tightly, and cook slowly for 20 minutes.

In a small bowl, combine powdered milk and sugar and stir in a little water to make a creamy paste. When smooth, add the rest of the water and vanilla. Stir into rice, cover, and simmer 10 minutes more or until flavors are blended. Chill or serve warm sprinkled lightly with cinnamon or nutmeg, if desired. Makes 4 servings.

NOTE: Recipe courtesy of Utah State University Extension.

APPLE KUCHEN

1 box	**yellow cake mix**
1/2 cup	**butter,** softened
1/2 cup	**shredded coconut**
1 can (20 ounces)	**apple pie filling**
1/2 cup	**sugar**
1 teaspoon	**cinnamon**
2 cups	**Powdered Milk Yogurt Sour Cream** (page 13) **or Powdered Milk Yogurt** (page 12)
1	**egg**

Preheat oven to 350 degrees.

In a large bowl, add cake mix and butter. Cut butter into cake mix until crumbly; mix in coconut. Pat into a 9 x 13-inch pan and bake for 10 minutes. Spread pie filling over crust and sprinkle with sugar and cinnamon.

In a medium bowl, mix sour cream and egg together until well combined and pour over filling. Return pan to oven and bake 25 minutes more, or until edges are golden brown. Makes 12–15 servings.

NOTE: Recipe courtesy of Tracey Lou Mullen.

FROZEN YOGURT

2 cups	**Powdered Milk Yogurt** (page 12)
1 cup	**water**
3 tablespoons	**powdered milk**
$1/4$ to $1/2$ cup	**flavored syrup,** of choice

Mix all ingredients together in a blender then freeze according to ice-cream freezer instructions. Makes 1 quart.

VARIATION: Replace water with 1 can (15 ounces) fruit of choice, with juice, and replace flavored syrup with $1/4$ to $1/2$ cup sugar, depending on fruit used.

LEMON FROZEN YOGURT

1 tablespoon	**lemon zest**
3/4 cup	**freshly squeezed lemon juice**
2 cups	**Powdered Milk Yogurt** (page 12)
1 cup	**sugar**
1/4 teaspoon	**salt**

Combine all ingredients in a medium bowl and mix well. Freeze according to ice-cream freezer instructions. Makes 1 quart.

CARAMEL

1/2 cup	**butter**
2 1/3 cups	**brown sugar**
1 cup	**white corn syrup**
1 3/4 cups	**Powdered Milk Sweetened Condensed Milk** (page 18)
1 teaspoon	**vanilla,** optional

Combine butter, brown sugar, and syrup in a medium saucepan. Stir well and bring to a boil over medium heat. Stir in condensed milk and vanilla, if using, and continue to cook, stirring constantly until mixture is at a soft ball stage, or until a soft strand forms when you drizzle some caramel into a cup of cold water. Makes approximately 3 cups.

NOTE: This is great for making caramel corn or caramel apples. Pour hot caramel over 3 gallons popped corn or cool slightly and dip 5–6 Granny Smith apples. It is also good used as a sauce drizzled over ice cream or bread puddings.

LICORICE CARAMELS

1 1/3 cup	**Powdered Milk Sweetened Condensed Milk** (page 18)
1 cup	**butter**
1 1/2 cups	**corn syrup**
2 cups	**sugar**
1/4 teaspoon	**salt**
1 tablespoon	**black food color paste**
1 bottle (.125 ounces)	**licorice oil**
1 bottle (.125 ounces)	**anise oil**

Combine condensed milk, butter, syrup, sugar, and salt in a large saucepan. Using a candy thermometer, cook and stir to 234 degrees or soft ball stage where a soft strand forms when you drizzle some caramel into a cup of cold water. Remove from heat and add food color paste and oils. Mix well. Pour into buttered 9 x 13-inch pan. Cool, then cut into 1-inch squares, and wrap in waxed paper. Makes approximately 120 pieces of candy.

FUDGE KISSES

1/2 cup	**butter,** softened
1/3 cup	**Powdered Milk Baker's Cheese** (page 22) **or Powdered Milk Yogurt Cream Cheese** (page 14)
1/3 cup	**cocoa powder**
1 pound	**powdered sugar**
1/2 teaspoon	**vanilla**

Combine all ingredients in a large bowl and mix well until color is consistent. Press mixture into a small funnel to shape into individual candies then wrap in aluminum foil or plastic wrap. You can add a small streamer with a message on it in the top of the wrap, if desired. Makes 12–24 candies.

VARIATION: You can add an almond in the center of each candy when you are forming the kisses.

PEANUT BUTTER FUDGE

4 cups	**sugar**
4 to 6 tablespoons	**cocoa powder**
6 tablespoons	**powdered milk**
2 cups	**water**
1 cup	**dark corn syrup**
1/2 cup	**butter**
1 cup	**peanut butter**
1 teaspoon	**vanilla**

Mix sugar, cocoa powder, and powdered milk together in a large saucepan. Stir in water and syrup. Bring to a boil over medium heat stirring with a wooden spoon. Boil until mixture forms a soft ball when dropped in water, about 30 minutes.

Take saucepan off the heat and stir in butter, peanut butter, and vanilla. Stir with wooden spoon until well mixed and fudge starts to set. Pour into buttered 8 x 8-inch pan, and smooth. Let cool, then cut into 1-inch pieces. Makes approximately 5 dozen pieces.

HINT: Butter the sides of your saucepan before you begin.

PEANUT BUTTER SESAME BALLS

1 cup	**peanut butter,** chunky or smooth
1 cup	**toasted sesame seeds**
1/2 cup	**honey**
1/4 cup	**powdered milk**
1/2 to 1 cup	**chopped nuts or dried fruit,** of choice

Mix all the ingredients together in a medium bowl until mixture is well blended and holds together. Shape into 1-inch balls and place on wax paper to set. Or press into a 4 x 8-inch pan and cut into squares. Keep refrigerated and store in an airtight container or ziplock bag. Makes approximately 36 balls.

PEANUT BUTTER CHEWS

>   1 cup **powdered sugar**
>   1 cup **powdered milk**
>   1 cup **peanut butter**
>   1 cup **corn syrup or honey**
>   2 cups **rice cereal, chopped nuts, or chocolate chips,** optional

In a large bowl, combine sugar and powdered milk; mix thoroughly. Mix peanut butter and syrup together in a small bowl and add to dry mixture. Add cereal or nuts, if using. Knead mixture with your hands until well combined, roll into balls, or press into an 8 x 8-inch pan and cut into 1-inch squares. Makes 5 dozen chews.

TOOTSIE ROLLS

2 tablespoons	**butter,** softened
2 squares	**Baker's chocolate,** melted*
3 cups	**powdered sugar**
3/4 cup	**powdered milk**
1/2 cup	**light corn syrup**
1 teaspoon	**vanilla,** or flavoring of choice

Combine all ingredients together in a large bowl and mix well. Roll into rolls and cut into bite-size pieces. Wrap in wax paper or plastic wrap. Makes 3–4 dozen rolls.

*Or 6 tablespoons cocoa powder and 2 tablespoons oil, mixed together.

HONEY MINTS

2³/₄ cups	**powdered milk**
1 cup	**warm honey**
4 drops	**oil of peppermint**
	food coloring, of choice

Mix ingredients together in a medium bowl and knead until thoroughly mixed. Roll into bite-size pieces and wrap in waxed paper or plastic wrap. Makes 2–3 dozen mints.

NOTES

NOTES

METRIC CONVERSION CHART

Volume Measurements

U.S.	Metric
1 teaspoon	5 ml
1 tablespoon	15 ml
1/4 cup	60 ml
1/3 cup	75 ml
1/2 cup	125 ml
2/3 cup	150 ml
3/4 cup	175 ml
1 cup	250 ml

Weight Measurements

U.S.	Metric
1/2 ounce	15 g
1 ounce	30 g
3 ounces	90 g
4 ounces	115 g
8 ounces	225 g
12 ounces	350 g
1 pound	450 g
2 1/4 pounds	1 kg

Temperature Conversion

Fahrenheit	Celsius
250	120
300	150
325	160
350	180
375	190
400	200
425	220
450	230

Yum! Check out these "101" favorites for more tasty recipes:

Apples	**More Cake Mix**
Bacon	**More Ramen**
BBQ	**More Slow Cooker**
Blender	**Potato**
Cake Mix	**Pancake Mix**
Canned Biscuits	**Peanut Butter**
Casserole	**Popcorn**
Chicken	**Pudding**
Chocolate	**Ramen Noodles**
Dutch Oven	**Rotisserie Chicken**
Eggs	**Slow Cooker**
Gelatin	**Toaster Oven**
Grits	**Tofu**
Ground Beef	**Tortilla**
Mac & Cheese	**Yogurt**
Meatballs	**Zucchini**

Each 128 pages, $9.99

Available at bookstores or
directly from GIBBS SMITH
1.800.835.4993
www.gibbs-smith.com
101yum.com

ABOUT THE AUTHOR

Darlene Carlisle has taught classes and workshops on uses of powdered milk for Utah State University Extension and church and community groups for a number of years. She lives in Utah.

Printed in the USA
CPSIA information can be obtained
at www.ICGtesting.com
LVHW021228050224
770978LV00007B/549